1992
The Facts
— and —
Challenges

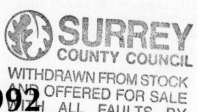
1992
The Facts
— and —
Challenges

by

Catherine
Taylor

and

Alison
Press

edited by Gina Marks

The Industrial Society

First published December 1988 by
The Industrial Society
Peter Runge House
3 Carlton House Terrace
London
SW1Y 5DG

ISBN 0 85290 402 9

Printed and bound in Great Britain by
Biddles Ltd, Guildford and King's Lynn

Acknowledgement

The Industrial Society should like to thank the following people for the writing of this publication:

Alison Press, a Research Associate with Ernst & Whinney, has worked in Brussels on an assignment for the Commission to produce brochures on 1992 and assists in producing material for Ernst & Whinney's clients.

Catherine Taylor, a consultant in the 1992 practice, works with Ernst & Whinney's clients in preparation for 1992.

Gina Marks is a Management Adviser with the Industrial Society who has special responsibility for the Society's campaign for 1992.

Contents

Foreword

It is a moot point whether a Single European Market for goods, services, labour and capital will arrive in 1992 or some years later, but there can be no doubt that it will happen in the 1990s. The issue is, will Britain approach it with enthusiasm, confidence and vision or will we muddle our way through, fearing the worst?

We need an integrated European policy on economic growth, unemployment, a flexible labour market and involvement of people in the workplace. It is only by having a united vision of what Europe can achieve against the competition of the USA, Japan and the newly industrialised countries on the Pacific rim, that we will bring about the change of attitudes which we need to win in the global marketplace.

The statistics which most illustrate Europe's lack of world competitiveness are the unemployment figures. In 1987, the European Community had 16 million unemployed, 11.7 per cent of the working population, compared to 6.7 per cent in the USA and 3.2 per cent in Japan.

Britain had shown the way in producing a more flexible labour market and while this is accompanied by high economic growth we can see unemployment falling. But we have to set alongside this optimistic picture our weaknesses in producing a highly trained workforce. This is nowhere more evident than among our managers.

When looking at labour force flexibility, both in skills and geographically, we should remember that most European countries will face a sharp drop in new recruits during the 1990s. We therefore have to invest in existing employees and not rely on a new generation to produce a competitive workforce.

We must also invest in language training if we are to compete effectively in the future. It is scandalous that children in our secondary schools can stop learning French at the end of their third year without having to take up another language.

Now that the common agricultural policy is fading as the only perspective from which British people see Europe, we must put a new vision before their eyes. We need a vision which enables us to overcome shared problems so we can all prosper from our increased ability to compete in world markets.

But we will only succeed if we bring the workforce into our confidence about the challenges of 1992 and what needs to be done to turn a possible threat into a major opportunity.

Catherine Taylor and Alison Press of Ernst & Whinney together with Gina Marks, the Industrial Society Europe Campaign Leader, have written an excellent book that lays down all of the facts and will allow all people in industry and commerce to face the challenges of 1992.

ALISTAIR GRAHAM
Director

Introduction

A year ago very few organisations would have been aware of the significance of "1992" and the Single European Market (SEM). Today, thanks to a vigorous awareness-raising campaign led by the Government, most people have heard of 1992. They know at least that 1992 is the date set by the European Commission (EC) for the completion of SEM. We hope that this book will be used as a guide to understanding what 1992 will really mean to people at work. It provides an understanding of the broad perspective with regard to the SEM and aims to make accessible to everyone what is an enormous and complex subject. We hope that the book's length and style will mean that everyone in an organisation will read it. More importantly we hope that everyone who reads it will come away with one message: "1992 means me" – for one thing is certain, that whatever you do and whoever you are, the SEM will have some impact on you.

Although there may still be some who are cynical about the prospects of success in completing the SEM, it is clear that 12 heads of government agreed, when they ratified the Single European Act 1987, to commit themselves to a changed Treaty of Rome thus ensuring that the SEM will be a reality. Our government, the French and the West German governments have invested heavily in large publicity campaigns to raise their respective industries' awareness of both the challenges and opportunities that 1992 will present them.

It should not be forgotten that the UK's closer integration with Europe will have profound psychological as well as practical effects. The completion of the SEM and the linking of the UK with the Continent of Europe in 1993 with the opening of the Channel Tunnel will entail organisations having to "think European" as never before. Organisations may well want to ensure that their most effective asset, their human resource – the people who make up the organisation – understand fully what the SEM is about and how it will impact on their company. The Industrial Society's Europe Campaign Department is ready to play an active part in this process and has a training package which will help organisations prepare for 1992.

Moreover on the language front, UK organisations that trade with the EC may well have to rethink their attitude to language training. Fifty per cent of our exports go to Europe – however research indicates that our exporters' potential is being damaged by lack of language skills. In the run-up to 1992 we must, in the context of an increasing number of cross-border mergers and takeovers, try to overcome our traditional resistance to learning foreign languages.

Whether it opens up opportunities for your organisation, threatens your domestic market or those of your suppliers, 1992 will have a deep impact on your organisation. In Appendix I we outline a checklist of key actions. If UK Limited is to rise to the challenge and meet the opportunities of 1992, we should not be caught unprepared. Now is the time for organisations to begin informing themselves and implementing strategic plans. The Industrial Society is grateful to Ernst & Whinney for their pioneering work and we hope that this book will prove to be both a valuable informative aid and a useful point of reference.

GINA MARKS
Europe Campaign Leader

1 The Background

Determined to lay the foundations of an ever-closer union among the peoples of Europe. Resolved to ensure the economic and social progress of their countries by common action to eliminate the barriers which divide Europe.

The Treaty of Rome, 1957

Treaty of Rome

The concept of a single European market is not a recent European Community (EC) development. In 1957, the Treaty of Rome was signed with the aim of creating a single integrated internal market. The reason for creating such an environment was to enable the European Community to prosper and function as a single political and economic unit. The Treaty laid out a programme to diminish the fragmentation of European markets. It envisaged reducing the following obstacles between Member States:

- the restricted movement of goods
- the inability of individuals to move freely
- the restrictions placed on selling services
- the restrictions on the free movement of capital
- the distortion of competition
- the differences in laws which impede a common market
- the varying levels of indirect tax.

Although a Common External Tariff was established, progress in achieving freedom of movement of goods, individuals, services and capital was slow, particularly hampered by the advent of a recession in the 1970s. Member States, faced with declining prosperity, implemented regulations to restrict access to their home market. This protectionism extended to the use of public funds for supporting national markets and industries. Clearly, this was not in the spirit of the Treaty of Rome.

The need to create a single economic environment was re-iterated in 1982 by the Commission and renewed energies are now being directed at achieving the aims of the Treaty. On a global level, competition is becoming increasingly intense. Even those Member States with high productivity find it difficult to compete globally. The Commission recognised that the only way in which to compete effectively with countries such as the USA and Japan was to complete the Single European Market. EC competitiveness relies on companies being able to operate across Europe, unimpeded by costly protectionist barriers.

Cost of Non-Europe

The failure to achieve a single market is costing Europe's industries millions. Earlier this year, the Commission published *1992 – The Benefits of a Single Market*, by Paolo Cecchini, the results of extensive research into the costs that a fragmented Europe produces for companies operating in the EC. The research addresses many areas, including:

- border-related controls
- technical standards
- public procurement practices
- the service sector.

Border-related controls

Ernst & Whinney undertook this particular research for inclusion in the above publication to determine the costs of customs procedures for intra-Community trade. The results show the cost of having to complete forms and the associated cost of delays incurred at customs points is approximately 2 per cent of an average consignment's value. The savings made by the introduction of a Single Administrative Document, replacing over one hundred different national trading forms is clearly a successful step in the Commission's programme to dismantle barriers. The cost of non-Europe to the road haulage industry must also be considered. The imposition by Member States of quotas and limits on collection and delivery by non-resident hauliers amounts to a cost of as much as £580 million per annum.

Technical standards

There are many problems which result from the divergences in technical standards and regulations which are in force in the Member States. The problems can be divided into those borne by:

PRODUCERS
- duplication of product development to meet national standards
- loss of economies of scale through the inability to produce for a single market
- disadvantages resulting from the need to focus on small national markets

NATIONAL GOVERNMENTS
- duplication of certification and testing costs
- achieving sub-optimal value for money in public purchasing

CONSUMERS
- a high proportion of the above costs being passed on to the final consumer.

Public procurement practices

Although public procurement is a huge market and therefore has considerable importance in the EC, only a tiny proportion of public purchasing is carried out across frontiers. Governments purchase from domestic firms, often paying higher prices than in other Member States. If public purchasing operated freely between Member States, it is estimated that as much as 17.5 billion ECU could be saved.

Services sector

Services are of growing importance in the European, as in the world, economy. However, nationally based services (particularly banking and insurance) are currently prevented from expanding to become Europe-wide through government regulations. Although these regulations, on the whole, were originally developed to protect consumers it is now the final consumer that bears the cost of a non-Europe in the services sector. Restricting competition can only lead to higher prices and poorer services for the consumer.

Added to these monetary costs of non-Europe are the opportunity costs in terms of companies being discouraged to expand on a pan-European basis. The savings that the EC can achieve through an integrated Europe could be diverted to new areas, creating increased wealth for the Community.

2 The European Commission's Objectives

The completion of the Internal Market is probably the most ambitious task that the Community has tackled since it was first set up. It will require courage and determination to carry out, but the rewards will be worthwhile.

Lord Cockfield – Vice President of the European Commission (from Commission booklet *Europe Without Frontiers, 1987*)

1985–The White Paper

A concrete commitment to the completion of an internal market was made with the publication of a Commission White Paper in June 1985. It contained a programme for action considered necessary to achieve a frontierless Europe and listed over 300 legislative proposals thought necessary to dismantle the obstacles which prevent the reality of a united Europe.

Existing Community policy must not be forgotten; it is intended that the Internal Market programme should work hand-in-hand with other areas of Community policy. The White Paper was followed by the adoption of the Single European Act in 1986, which speeded up the process of decision making. The Act amended the Treaty of Rome to allow legislative measures to be adopted by a majority vote, replacing the previous requirements for a unanimous vote.

Regional policy

If goods, individuals, services and capital are free to move around the Community it is likely that resources will flow out of some areas and into others. This has obvious implications for the Community's regional policy; the distribution of funds will have to be reconsidered.

Agricultural policy

Much of the administration for the Common Agricultural Policy is carried out at the borders. If these are truly to disappear then alternative arrangements will have to be made.

Internal frontiers

It is the Commission's aim to remove all internal frontiers within the Community by 1992 – not an easy task when we consider the multitude of purposes they serve:

- monitoring entry and exit of travellers
- controlling movements of terrorists, criminals, illegal immigrants
- collecting VAT and excise duties
- compiling trade statistics
- monitoring health standards by plant and animal checks.

It is the underlying rationale of the internal borders which must be tackled – a task that will bring into question many nationalistic ideals. In the quest for a unified market, questions of public security and health must not be relegated to second place; instead these issues must be faced on a Community-wide rather than a national basis.

To achieve its objective of a truly Common Market the Commission's White Paper identified three areas where action would be necessary to complete the Single European Market:

- physical barriers
- technical barriers
- fiscal barriers.

Physical barriers

Of all the obstacles to a free Europe it is the physical barriers, such as border posts within the Community, that are the most visible. These border controls are a source of continual frustration for travellers and for those who import/export throughout Europe.

The Commission's aim is that eventually Community citizens will be able to travel freely through Europe with the use of a European passport and "fast" channels at ports/airports/border crossings. Individuals will still be subject to spot checks but, on the whole, travel will be much easier.

However, for this to be a success there have to be:

- tighter controls at external borders
- a common approach to terrorism, criminals, drugs etc
- a common policy for the treatment of non-Europeans – immigration, visa requirements etc.

The Single Administrative Document

The passage of goods across borders has been simplified greatly with the introduction of the Single Administrative Document (SAD) at the beginning of this year. Mountains of paperwork have disappeared, but there is still much to be done.

Agricultural checks

Borders are a convenient place for the calculation of Monetary Compensation Amounts (MCAs) which are applied under the Common Agricultural Policy (CAP). Hopefully, these will be phased out in the near future, but if this proves to be an impossible task then they will have to be administered away from the borders.

Health checks

Different national health regulations for animals and plants (eg rabies in the UK) result in extensive checking at borders. Here the Commission's objective is to formulate common policies on health checks which will be observed throughout the Community so that restrictions will no longer be necessary.

Transport

Most intra-Community transport is subject to quotas – limiting the number of journeys that lorries can undertake in other (and sometimes their own) Member States. Consequently, journey authorisations are subject to stringent checks at frontiers. It has now been agreed that these will be progressively relaxed.

Technical barriers

It is not only border posts that hamper free movement across frontiers. A variety of technical "under-the-surface" barriers also exist, preventing the free movement of people and services.

Goods

The maintenance of different product regulations – whether motivated by health, safety or environmental considerations – has the effect of preventing goods moving freely between European States. Manufacturers are often forced to produce 12 varieties of their products in order to be able to market them Europe-wide. Different checks have to be carried out in the individual Member States to ensure compliance with the relevant national standards.

The Commission does not aim to adopt a European standard for all components of all products. Instead, it is only "essential health and safety requirements" that will be harmonised, combined with a "mutual recognition" of other standards/regulations. Thus a product which is passed as fit to be marketed in one Member State will be permitted in all others without further checks.

People

It is not only border controls that stop individuals living and working where they want to in Europe, either. For example, educational and professional qualifications gained in one Member State may not be recognised in another – a considerable obstacle to setting up where you choose. The Commission's aim is to ensure that there is mutual recognition of such qualifications.

Services

The services industry is becoming increasingly important in the developed economies, yet in many areas it is virtually impossible to provide services across frontiers. Many sectors suffer, including:

- banking
- insurance
- transport
- telecommunications.

It is generally the *consumer* who suffers most by the lack of competition, even though, ironically, many of the protectionist regulations were originally designed for consumer protection.

The approach

Previously, lengthy negotiations to harmonise product regulations between the Member States proved an almost impossible procedure. Now the approach is to harmonise only essential health and safety regulations and combine these with a mutual recognition of other regulations and standards. The complex and enormous amount of legislation that would be necessary to harmonise all standards is avoided, and consumers *will* still have a choice.

Fiscal barriers

These present probably the largest and most difficult obstacle to a united market, even though they lurk below the surface. The differences in indirect taxation preserve the need for border posts – VAT is refunded on export, payable on import. Often, large differences in VAT between the Member States make this a financially worthwhile exercise. Abolition of border controls may encourage fraud, so differences in VAT levels would have to be sufficiently small to make smuggling a pointless exercise.

The benefits

The maintenance of a fragmented Europe is obviously detrimental to all its citizens. The benefits that will accrue from a united Europe will be immense with individuals being free to move around as they please, living and working where they choose.

Customer choice will be increased, and heightened competition will result in better customer service. Businesses will be compelled to widen their horizons and recognise that their domestic market consists of 12 nations, not one. Manufacturing plants will be located in areas which provide the greatest return. There will be a greater choice of finance, insurance and the like. Everyone will benefit, but only if they inform themselves of the changes to come, recognise the opportunities and rise to the challenge.

3 How to Lobby in the Community

At present, approximately one-third of the proposed legislative measures put forward by the European Commission have been adopted by the Council of Ministers, so the Single European Market is by no means a *fait accompli*. It is intended that the completion of the Single Market should benefit everyone; something that can be facilitated if the European law makers know the views and opinions of European citizens. To know how you can make your views known it is essential to understand how the legislative process works.

The different organs of power

There are five particularly important power groups within the Community, all of which play a part in the legislative process:

● European Commission
● European Parliament
● Economic and Social Committee
● Council of Ministers
● European Court of Justice.

The European Commission

The Commission has been described as "the guardian of the

11

Treaties which set up the European Community". In line with this role it is responsible for proposing Community policy and handling Community administration. It has 17 members chosen by the governments of the Member States; each Member State must have at least one representative but not more than two. Commissioners are obliged to act in the Community's interest, something which does not always make them popular with their national governments. The administrative side of the Commission is made up of 22 Directorates-General – DGs – each of which have specific areas of responsibility. For example, DG I is responsible for external relations; DG III is responsible for the Internal Market; DG VI is responsible for agriculture.

It is the Commission's job to produce proposals for legislation which are then discussed further down the line.

The European Parliament

This is the only directly elected organ of the Community. It has three main areas of power:

- legislative – the right to be consulted and to make amendments to any legislation proposed by the Commission
- financial – the right to request changes in expenditure and reject the Community budget
- control – the right to question both the Council and the Commission, and take either to the Court of Justice.

There are several committees within the Parliament covering specific areas of Community activity, eg Agriculture, Transport, Legal Affairs.

The Economic and Social Committee (ECOSOC)

This is an advisory and consultative committee which was set up to ensure that all groups of people were involved in the Community's decision-making processes. The Committee must be consulted by the Council or the Commission in several areas of Community policy. It has 189 members representing workers and employers and various interest groups such as consumers and the professions.

The Council of Ministers

The Council is the only Community institution which directly represents the governments of the Member States. Each Member State has one seat. It is the Council which has the power to adopt Community legislation, although this is generally conditional upon a proposal being tabled by the Commission. Prior to 1986 and the adoption of the Single European Act, all Council decisions had to be unanimous. However, the Single European Act, which was adopted to facilitate the creation of a single market, amends the Treaties which set up the Community, allowing majority voting in certain circumstances.

The European Court of Justice

It is the Court of Justice's responsibility to determine the correct interpretation of Community law. It settles disputes between the Member States and has the power to impose fines. Each Member State is represented by a judge.

The process of law making

This is most easily depicted in a diagram (see Appendix II). Essentially it is a three-stage process.

- The Commission drafts a proposal which it submits to the Council.
- The Parliament and the Economic and Social Committee (ECOSOC) consider the proposal and formulate an opinion. The Parliament may request the Commission to make amendments to its proposal.

- The Council of Ministers adopts the proposal which then becomes law.

This is known as the Consultation Procedure. Following the adoption of the Single European Act a slightly different procedure may be followed:

- The Commission produces a proposal as before which is submitted to the Council.
- The Economic and Social Committee and the Parliament again have the opportunity for comment.
- The Council, taking the opinions of the Parliament and ECOSOC into account, then formulates a "common position" and the proposal is returned to the Parliament for a second reading.
- If the Parliament agrees with the Council's common position then it may adopt the proposal by qualified majority voting. If it does not, the proposal may only be adopted by unanimity.

This is known as the Co-operation Procedure which aims to give the Parliament a louder voice and speed up the process of decision making by allowing majority voting.

The different types of legislative measures

There are essentially four different sorts of legislative measures:

- regulations
- directives
- decisions
- recommendations.

The majority of measures in the 1992 programme are Council Directives.

REGULATIONS
A regulation is a law which is binding on all Member States. No

action need be taken by the Member States to implement any national legislation. Regulations can be adopted by both the Council of Ministers and the Commission.

DIRECTIVES
A Directive imposes on Member States a certain result to be achieved but leaves the method up to the individual Member States. Generally speaking, each Member State has to introduce some legislation of its own to comply with the Directive. The impact of national legislation is included in the consideration of the effects of a Directive.

DECISIONS
Similar to a regulation, a decision is binding on those to whom it is addressed. Again, both the Council and the Commission have the power to adopt decisions.

RECOMMENDATIONS
A recommendation is not a law and hence has no binding effect on any of the Member States.

So where do you fit in?

As you can see from the diagrams in Appendix II, the Commission's proposals have to go through several stages before they can become law, so there is plenty of opportunity for individuals to make themselves heard.

- A first stage is a lobbying of the Commission before draft proposals are produced. This can be done directly, through one of the lobbying organisations that exist solely for this purpose or through trade associations, Chambers of Commerce and the like. The DTI are releasing the names of civil servants in the UK who can provide assistance in particular areas. Further information as to whom to contact can be obtained from the DTI (address in Appendix IV).
- An obvious route is via the European Parliament. Members of the European Parliament (MEPs) are directly elected by us and therefore have a duty to represent our views if they are made

known to them. To find out who your local MEP is telephone the UK office of the European Parliament (address given in Appendix IV).

- The Economic and Social Committee is of particular importance to businesses; one-third of its members are representatives of employers.
- The European Trade Union Confederation was created in 1973 solely for the purpose of representing the views and interests of European workers.
- The Committee of Permanent Representatives (COREPOR) is another route through which views may be channelled. It is from this Committee that a working party is formed to examine the Commission's proposals on behalf of the Council.

The Single European Market should make life better for all Europeans provided their views are made known to the organisations that make the decisions.

How to seek redress where unfair barriers to trade remain

If an individual or an organisation believes that Community rules are working unfairly, then it is open to these individuals or organisations (be they governments, local authorities, companies or individuals) to complain to the European Court of Justice and seek redress. The DTI's booklet *The Single Market: Europe Open For Business* describes the criteria for making a complaint and the procedures as follows:

"The EEC Treaty, in particular Article 30, establishes the principle that Member States cannot maintain quantitative restrictions, or measures which have the equivalent effect, on products from other Member States. These rules apply directly in all Member States. They apply equally to measures by central and local government, and by regulatory bodies set up or supported by governments to carry out government policy.

The European Court of Justice (ECJ) has also laid down broad guidelines that any rules 'enacted by Member States which are capable of hindering, directly or indirectly, actually or potentially, intra-Community trade' are covered by Article 30. The measures prohibited include any discrimination between home produced and foreign goods, onerous technical standards, or testing procedures, burdensome labelling requirements, unequal taxation regimes, over-rigid pricing or profit margin controls, requirements for import licences or similar procedures, and many other obstacles.

There are some limited exceptions to the general principle of free movement: governments can, for instance, restrict the flow of some goods on grounds of public morality, safety, the protection of health and life of humans, animals or plants. But the exceptions must not constitute a disguised restriction on trade, and the ECJ has generally ruled in favour of the free movement of goods. (For instance, they recently judged illegal German laws on beer purity dating from the sixteenth century.)

The Commission is working on an inventory of the budget resources which Member States use for state subsidies. This should be completed in 1988. The results will give the Commission a much better base on which to judge the extent to which they have been able to regulate existing support, and enable them to identify and take action against subsidies which are being granted without approval.

By 1992 the Commission plans to have tightened its implementation of the rules so that state funding is not used to confer artificial and unjustified advantages on some Community firms over others. This is essential if subsidies are not to be used to replace barriers to trade as effective obstacles to free and fair competition."

There can be no mistake, therefore, that the UK Government is committed to the Commission's efforts to ensure the fair application of rules throughout the EC. The DTI is prepared to take up cases of unfair barriers to trade where UK firms face them in other Member States. It can do this both by taking action with other Member States' governments and with the Commission. According to the DTI, it will also intervene before the European Court of Justice when major national interests are at stake. The DTI has stated in the same publication that if you are facing unfair trading practices of the type described above, you should contact them to see what they can do to help. The contact address is:

Internal European Policy Division
Department of Trade and Industry
Room 405
1–19 Victoria Street
London SW1H 0ET.

4 What Does 1992 Mean to Industry?

The legislative programme to complete the Single European Market is a process as opposed to a watershed and industry cannot afford to ignore it. There are three aspects to the evolutionary process of the legislative programme:

- the fact that legislation has been proposed and adopted since the inception of the Treaty of Rome
- the fact that legislation is being updated in the light of the new technology, scientific discoveries and changes in the market place, and
- the fact, as mentioned in Chapter 3, that UK industry can still play a vital role in determining the final shape of legislation, some of which is still in its early stages.

The legislative programme

Frontier controls

The Commission intends to remove frontier controls (see Chapter 2) and customs procedures. These formalities largely derive from differences in technical standards, exchange controls, health and safety regulations, indirect tax regimes between Member States as well as concern to prevent the movement of illegal arms, terrorists, drugs and pornography. By promoting the maximum possible harmonisation and mutual recognition of controls between Member States, it is hoped eventually to abolish frontier controls within the Community.

Financial services and capital movement

The aim is to allow banks, building societies and insurance companies established in one Member State to establish branches and sell services in all the others. The regulatory changes include some harmonisation (eg of the form of published accounts, reserve ratios) and the principles of mutual recognition and home country control and the introduction of a single banking licence, the latter meaning that the bank established in one Member State and therefore subject to supervision there, should be free to establish subsidiaries throughout the Community without needing approval in the "host" countries. To make these developments a reality, foreign exchange controls on capital movements by individuals and companies are to be abolished.

An example of how much it costs currently to move capital around the Member States was graphically demonstrated by a leading European Community Consumers Organisation.* An exercise was carried out by telephone, starting with BFr 40,000 (£613.00) and working clockwise through the EC via the UK, France and Spain, and back again. They ended up with just BFr 21,300 or 47 per cent less!

It is hoped that the current demands made on financial institutions establishing subsidiaries in other Member States will be significantly reduced through the introduction of, for example, a single banking licence. This will permit a bank to undertake a wide range of activities, throughout the Community, provided that they are permitted in the bank's home country. These activities will be regulated under home country control. A UK bank's subsidiary in Turin will be supervised by the Bank of

*Holiday Money; BEUC, Rue Royale 29, Boite 3, B–1000 Brussels, Belgium.

England, for example. The hope is that individuals and companies will be free to open accounts throughout the Community.

The Commission recognises, however, the need to strike a balance between:

- creating a single market for financial services and capital
- the need to ensure consumer and investor protection
- the need for Member States to pursue national monetary policies.

Standards for food, drink, pharmaceuticals and other manufactured goods

There are currently 12 different sets of national technical standards covering food additives, colourings, packaging, pharmaceutical testing and pricing, technical standards for a wide variety of engineering products from motor car "type approval" to specifications for elevators, and health and safety regulations for goods such as tractors and toys. A major programme of reform is under way to set harmonised standards in health and safety and to open up markets on the basis of mutual recognition.

European standards are being established by the European standards bodies CEN and CENELEC. These consist of over 100 committees which, at present, are dominated by French and German representatives. UK businesses will have to increase their presence in these committees to ensure that their concerns are included.

Livestock, fruit and vegetables

Differences in national standards relating to the inspection and control of trade in animals, meat, fish, vegetables and fruit inhibit trade, slow down transit across frontiers, and make trade more costly.

The aim is to remove checks and controls at borders by an ambitious programme of harmonisation of regulations and greater reliance on certification issued at the point of departure.

Telecommunications and transport

Currently, the fragmentation of broadcasting and information services by national controls and the existence of different technical specifications reduce Europe's ability to compete in world markets by reducing the attractiveness of research and development on a sufficient scale. The aim is to reduce controls on cross-border telecommunications traffic and to introduce Community-wide technical standards for television, portable telephones and information technology and telecommunication equipment. Measures are being proposed to facilitate pan-European satellite broadcasting. This includes proposals on the content of television advertising, to protect audiences such as children.

In the case of transport, competition is limited by air fare and capacity sharing deals, national quotas on foreign coach and lorry operators, and restrictions on water-borne freight movement. The aim is to liberalise the market in all these areas.

Electronic data management

A major programme has been initiated by the Commission to encourage the use of "Trade Electronic Data Interchange Systems" throughout the Community. Electronic Data Interchange (EDI) enables companies to reduce dramatically administration costs associated with order and invoice processing as well as facilitating day-to-day trading relationships across great distances.

Public procurement

Purchases by government and nationalised industries account for over 10 per cent of Gross Domestic Product (GDP) in the average Member State. However, up till now the markets for public construction projects, telecommunications, energy, water, transport, office equipment and a host of other goods and services have tended to be restricted to domestic suppliers. It is proposed to open up these markets to all EC Member States and means of ensuring compliance with this requirement are being examined. Large procurement contracts will have to be published across the

Community allowing other EC Member States' companies to tender for the work.

In addition, to assist small and medium sized enterprises (SMEs), a database is being developed to enable them to undertake sub-contracting work for public procurement contracts. Details of this are in Appendix IV.

Trade marks

The existence of twelve different trade-mark systems is intended to be replaced by a Community-wide system.

Company law

The creation of cross-frontier companies and of joint ventures is to be encouraged by changes in company law. These include the creation of a new legal entity, a "European Economic Interest Grouping" which will benefit companies which do not wish to merge or form joint subsidiaries, but wish to carry out certain activities in common. Joint projects for research and development, and joint marketing of complementary products, are two examples of such activities.

In addition, the Commission proposes to create a European company with its own legislative framework, which will allow companies incorporated in different Member States to merge, to form a holding company or a joint subsidiary without suffering from conflicting national laws.

The Commission has also tabled proposals on the corporate structure of public limited liability companies to ensure that they are effectively supervised on behalf of shareholders. Proposals have also been tabled to ensure that there is employee participation in the management of these companies. The present proposal on worker participation has been under discussion since 1972. As it is politically controversial, many amendments have been included. The extent to which worker participation will be legally required is currently under review. Although the effect could cause major changes in the way that UK firms operate, the Commission has recently revised some of the proposals to enable national governments more freedom on the extent to which they implement the directive. This directive has not yet been approved. For more information about the fifth Directive and the so-called "Vredeling directive" on worker participation, see Julia Middleton's *Consultation* (The Industrial Society 1986, London).

Taxation

Eventually, it is hoped to harmonise corporation tax systems so that investment decisions by companies are not affected by tax considerations. This will also dramatically reduce the penalties, such as double taxation, currently incurred by companies with subsidiaries in other Member States.

In addition, the Commission plans to narrow the differences in VAT and Excise Duties regimes across Member States. This is one of the most politically sensitive proposals, as VAT varies widely across the Community. The current proposals provide for two bands of VAT. The aim is to dismantle fully the fiscal frontiers by approximating VAT rates and unifying excise duties, which should mean that administrative border controls are no longer necessary.

Depending on the outcome of continuing discussions, some UK products currently zero rated (such as children's clothes) could become liable for VAT payments.

Vocational qualifications and professional services

It is intended to promote the mutual recognition by all member states of a wide range of educational, technical and professional qualifications awarded in one country. This will mean that those with such qualifications will be freer than at present to seek employment across the Community. It will also mean that firms offering professional services, in particular, will have greater freedom to operate across the Community and will be able to set up their brass plates freely across the Community.

Related wider issues

Merger policies

In parallel with the proposals specifically intended to create a single Community market, the Commission is taking a more active role in merger policy. The Commission has powers to review and, if necessary, to reverse mergers which have Community-wide implications for competition. The Commission has more recently tabled proposals to enable it to vet mergers before the event.

At the same time, the Commission recognises the need to promote the development of Community-based companies to undertake research, development and production on the scale necessary to compete more effectively in world markets.

Trade with non-EC 'third' countries

As the Community moves towards a single market without frontier controls, it will become increasingly difficult and inappropriate to maintain separate national quotas on imports – of such things as cars, clothing, electronics goods and textiles – from non-EC countries. It seems likely that the firms which receive the most protection from non-EC imports will face stiffer competition. The Community as a whole will take on an increasingly important role in negotiating with third countries and will be in a more powerful position than individual Member States to open up markets in third countries.

Companies from non-EC countries

Companies from a large number of third countries and a wide variety of sectors currently have establishments in, and do business with, the Community. The proposals for the creation of a single European market have major implications for such companies. The Nestle take-over of Rowntree Mackintosh is an example of a company from a non-Community country buying into a successful company in an EC Member State. It will thus be ready to take advantage of Europe's single domestic market of 320 million people. The freedom of access to Community markets will also depend on the outcome of negotiations over reciprocal rights between their national authorities and the Community. At present the requirement for reciprocal rights only appears in the banking and investment services directives.

Opportunities outside the Community

It should be clear that the outcome of negotiations with third countries over import quotas and reciprocal rights for Community and non-Community companies will have major implications for Community-based companies:

- in terms of their opportunities to export to third countries, and
- in terms of their ability to establish operations in such countries

so that the creation of a single European market affects world-wide business and is not confined to the 12 Member States.

Impact on industry sectors

The following list of industry sectors are those most likely to be affected by regularity changes:

- high technology and telecommunications
- pharmaceuticals and chemicals
- food and drink
- manufacturing
- transport
- construction
- retailing
- professions.

High technology and telecommunications

The Community telecommunications market is currently fragmented both in terms of products and services.

The Commission's proposals to widen the public procurement supplier market, in conjunction with the Europeanisation of national service regulations and technical standards should provide great opportunities. In addition, Post, Telephone and Telecommunications Services (PTTs) across the Community will be urged to become more commercial, along the lines of British Telecom.

The Commission's proposals should result in greater compatibility and interoperability between European computer systems. There will also be savings due to the harmonisation of technical standards and specifications. The national monopolies for the supply of equipment to PTTs will be broken down, giving third countries as well as other Member States access to these previously protected markets.

The Commission is also providing financial incentives for transfrontier joint ventures for research and development (R & D). The ability to compete at a global level depends very much on EC-scale investment in research and development.

Manufacturers and suppliers of services in this industry sector may be able to market equipment and services on a pan-European level.

Pharmaceuticals and chemicals

The current drug licensing and pricing differences partition national Community markets. The Commission aim to create an EC market through legislation resulting in:

- a multi-state application procedure for drug licensing
- harmonised drug testing, licensing, packaging and pricing
- the limited marketing of dangerous goods.

In addition, public authorities, including publicly financed health services, will be opening up their contracts to non-national suppliers. Third countries outside the Community may gain market share as a result of this. There should be opportunities for:

- pan-European tendering
- pan-European sales and marketing
- faster recoupment of R & D costs as the licensing process is accelerated.

Food and drink

The harmonisation of sampling, analysis, food content, packaging and marketing, together with the harmonisation of health controls on animals and plants and narrowing the differences in VAT regimes and excise duties, are likely to have a considerable impact on this sector.

Companies should experience greater access to other Member States' consumers. Exciting opportunities should also be created by the increased ability for European branding, packaging and marketing. However, it should be noted that the likely restructuring of the food sector could be undertaken by better positioned non-EC countries.

The drinks sector will be most affected by the changes due in VAT and excise duties. Cost to the consumer will be less disparate than currently.

Manufacturing

The following 1992 legislation will make an impact on manufacturing based companies:

- harmonisation of technical standards and specifications
- reduction in restrictive public procurement practices in telecommunications, pharmaceuticals, energy, transport and water sectors
- approximation of indirect tax (VAT)
- limitation of state funding for national industries.

Manufacturers should benefit from increased opportunities for:

- economies of scale

- cross-frontier R & D, partly funded by the Commission
- improved competitiveness in tendering for public procurement contracts
- European stock management.

Inefficient manufacturers currently protected by nationalistic practices will face increasing competition.

Transport

The Commission's central policy on transport aims to liberalise transport services throughout Europe. Following the first stage of liberalising transport services across Member States, the second phase aims to liberalise transport within Member States. The result of these deregulation measures should produce:

- access to new markets and cabotage limitations (the practice of allowing foreign transport to unload goods only) being phased out
- cost savings in terms of reduced documentation requirements and delays for road hauliers
- increased competition, particularly in air services and air fares
- opportunities to create European distribution networks.

However, it may be that powerful third country operators, particularly in the air carrier sector, may stimulate defensive mergers and acquisitions.

Construction

The harmonisation of standards will have a limited effect in this sector. More significant, however, is the potential impact of the public procurement directives which will result in public construction projects being open to non-national suppliers. The Commission expects these regulatory changes to provide opportunities for the formation of pan-European consortia for public procurement contracts.

Retailing

Retailing of products and services is directly and indirectly affected by the 1992 legislative programme. The harmonisation of standards will require European-style labelling and packaging. The deregulation of road haulage and the easing of customs controls will impact on distribution. The trend, supported by the Commission, towards electronic payment systems will continue. There may be opportunities for:

- economies of scale through retailing to larger markets than the national one
- acquisitions and mergers to gain distribution networks
- strategic relocation of warehouses and distribution points
- strengthening links with transport companies.

Professions

The Commission have agreed proposals to promote the mutual recognition of a wide range of educational, technical and professional qualifications awarded in one Member State by all other Member States. Individuals with qualifications will be freer to seek employment across the Community. Firms offering professional services in particular will have greater freedom to operate across the Community. The value of linguistic skills, particularly in the UK, will be increased.

Impact on business functions

We now turn to the following specific business functions, where the impact of the regulatory changes is likely to be particularly significant:

- human resources
- training
- recruitment methods

- corporate objective setting
- research and development
- distribution
- finance and accounting
- marketing and production
- public relations
- purchasing.

Human resources

Organisations may wish to establish a 1992 resource, with an appointed member of staff monitoring the 1992 developments. On a more general level, training in languages and cultures may be required for staff in companies using 1992 as a platform to enter the Community market.

Arguably English is the acknowledged language of trade. Nevertheless, organisations willing to invest in language training may reap the benefits. The value of having personnel with the ability not only to negotiate successfully in a customer's language but who are also sensitive to cultural differences will be enormous, eg. switchboard operators with linguistic skills (most large companies in Europe have such operators). Recruiting practices may change in response to the facility to recruit across borders. Personnel procedures may also have to change in response to Directives addressed to harmonising the social aspects of the Community.

Training

Generally, to meet the high quality of service and manufactured goods that are produced by the mainland, UK employees need to understand the increased competitive environment. Impending changes, and the reasons for them, need to be communicated down the line. Communication procedures should be improved if necessary. Organisations should review their training programmes in light of the Single European Market.

Recruitment methods

Procedures may also need to be reviewed and restructured.

31

Mutual recognition of both professional and vocational qualifications may widen an organisation's target recruitment field.

Corporate objective setting

1992 has provided many Community companies with an impetus for change. Changes in the marketplace may require you to redefine your objectives to exploit identified new opportunities. Even if your company is operating in the UK alone, national and international competitors may be encroaching on your market. Corporate objectives should take this into account.

Research and development

Changing requirements for standards and specifications may impact on R & D activities. In addition, the Commission's financial incentives for cross-frontier R & D ventures could provide opportunities for funded projects.

Distribution

The liberalisation of the transport industry should provide opportunities for more centralised European warehousing and distribution points. There should also be more competitive options in choosing distributors.

Finance and accounting

For companies operating in more than one Member State, the Commission is proposing to relieve some of the burden of reporting and accounting required to meet varying national standards.

Marketing and production

Strategic positioning of products and services may have to be reconsidered not only in the light of new opportunities but also of emerging new threats.

Production of goods may be affected by the changes in technical standards.

Public relations

1992 is a useful public relations tool. There may be opportunities to exploit 1992 as a vehicle for change.

Purchasing

Your suppliers may be affected by the changing environment. You might find new, cheaper sources for raw materials and other supplies.

5 Small and Medium-sized Enterprises

A single market creates an enormous challenge for the smaller company. We want to convert that challenge into an opportunity. There is a danger we will create a large market with no place for the smaller firm.

Abel Matutes – Commissioner with responsibility for small businesses, quoted in the *Financial Times* on 22 March 1988.

The problem

From 1 January 1993 we shall have a Europe where goods, people and services can move easily across frontiers. Everyone will have to 'think big' – after all, the 'domestic' market will consist of approximately 320 million people.

As consumers are offered more choice, competition will be tough; a new variety and a lower price will be necessary to win orders. It is likely that we will see a vast number of mergers and/or hostile takeovers as individual companies seek to tighten their grasp on this market of 320 million consumers.

It is feasible that in each market sector we will have just a few, very large, pan-European companies, leaving no room for the smaller private (or public) companies.

The Commission's response

The Commission recognises the importance of Small and Medium-sized Enterprises (SMEs) for job creation and innovation, and for this reason it wants to see their continued existence after 1992. The Commission is well aware of the dangers facing small businesses and it is taking action to prevent them being swallowed up by large conglomerates.

The first step came in 1983 – European Small Business Year – which aimed to bring the importance of small businesses to everyone's notice. The Commission then proposed an action programme for SMEs which was approved by the Council of Ministers in October 1986. Abel Matutes, a Spanish businessman, was appointed Commissioner with responsibility for small businesses. In order to implement this action programme, the Commission created a special unit – the SME Task Force – which is discussed in more detail below.

The Commission has often stressed that this action programme is not designed to create privileges for smaller businesses. Rather, it is intended to create favourable social and economic conditions for all companies, having a particular impact on smaller companies with limited resources.

The SME Task Force

Created in 1986, the Task Force was set up to help smaller businesses become informed about and hence prepared for 1992. It is headed up by Alan Mayhew – an economist who has worked for the Commission since 1974. It has a staff of about 40 based in Brussels. Its aim is to work side by side with national agencies already established in the Member States.

Probably the most important work done by the Task Force is to carry out an assessment of the impact that all new Community legislation will have on the smaller business. It is the Task Force's job to ensure that disproportionate financial or administrative burdens do not fall on small businesses with limited resources. It also presses the law makers to consult all relevant trade associations, employers' organisations, and so on, before tabling any legislation.

Another important aspect of the Task Force's work is to ensure that all SMEs are adequately informed. It has several channels for disseminating information:

- Euro-Info Bulletin
- Target 1992
- Euro-Info Centres
- Business – Co-operation Network (B–C Net).

Euro-Info Bulletin

Produced approximately six times a year, this is mailed free of charge to all smaller businesses, keeping them up to date with events in the Commission which have particular relevance for the smaller company.

Target 1992

This is a monthly newsletter on the Single European Market, published jointly by the Task Force and the unit for information, communication and culture. It provides information on the 1992 programme with small businesses in mind.

Euro-Info Centres

There are now 39 of these centres throughout the Community, four of which are in the UK. They form a vital interface between businessmen and the Commission, providing advice and answering questions on all aspects of the Single European Market. The 39 centres are linked to the Commission and to each other by means of an electronic database.

Business – Co-operation Network (B–C Net)

This is to be a computerised network system that will eventually link small businesses with each other, with business consultants, with accountants, with banks, development agencies and the like. The aim is to promote co-operation between these various players so they can join forces and compete with larger companies on an equal footing.

What has been achieved so far?

Some special advantages have already arisen for SMEs out of the 1992 programme:

- VAT
- SAD
- Single Person Company.

VAT

The Commission has produced a proposal to amend a previous VAT Directive which introduces a simplified system for SMEs and raises the thresholds for exemption from the system. If approved by the Council of Ministers, a vast number of SMEs could be excluded from the VAT system.

SAD

The introduction of the Single Administrative Document is likely to benefit the SMEs most of all. It will benefit all Community importers/exporters but will be particularly important for the smaller company where administrative costs are proportionately higher than for larger companies.

Single Person Company

A proposal is currently under consideration setting out a legal framework for a single person company. The Commission sees this as a way of encouraging enterprise and initiative in individuals without a personal financial liability. If approved by the Council it could allow individuals to set up on their own, without needing the backing of other shareholders, while limiting their liability to the value of their personal equity.

What is expected in the future?

There are several areas where action is awaited in the 1992 programme which will be of particular importance to SMEs:

- research and development
- public procurement
- European financing company.

Research and development

There are currently several European programmes aimed at promoting R & D within the Community, eg SPRINT, BRITE, ESPRIT. At present these are for large projects; a representative value being ECU 2 million (£1,400,000). These are of no help to smaller companies since they have neither the time nor the financial resources to spend three months writing a proposal and looking for partners in the project. It is hoped that some of the contracts can be split into smaller projects worth, say, ECU 250,000, which is a far more realistic value to allow smaller firms to participate.

Public procurement

Smaller companies often find themselves excluded from the competition for public supply contracts because of the sheer size and complexity of the market. The Directives currently in force concerning public procurement only require contracts over a certain value to be put out to open tender. National governments try to get round the rule by splitting their contracts into small parts which then do not need to be put out to tender. As a result SMEs do not have a chance to compete for those contracts that would be suitable. It is the Commission's aim to improve the transparency of this market, improve information flows, and allow all companies (especially the smaller ones) to have equal access. This will be achieved for SMEs via the B–C Net.

European financing company

The Commission is helping with the start-up of a company whose aim is to provide financial support to the cross-frontier co-operation of smaller companies. An initiative concerned with venture capital is also under consideration. The Commission is promoting the growth of Unlisted Securities Markets across the Community as another route for smaller companies to find finance.

The SME is one of the most vulnerable players in the economy as the reality of the Single Market approaches. It is, therefore, vital that each small company makes itself aware of:

- the changes to come
- the pitfalls to avoid
- the opportunities to grasp.

6 Preparing for 1992

The overriding message is:

DON'T BE COMPLACENT!

Management cannot afford to ignore the moves to complete the Single European Market because:

- some changes are mandatory if organisations want to stay in business
- competitors may be ahead of you in assessing 1992
- some implications should be considered to protect your current markets
- some implications should be considered to take advantage of new opportunities.

Managers need to ensure that they grasp the opportunities now to meet the challenges of the creation of the Single European Market.

STEP 1: Be aware of legislation

Commission legislation, intended to remove barriers to trade, is constantly being formulated and needs to be monitored. Many companies have allocated particular members of staff specific responsibilities to keep track of legislation and instigate lobbying where necessary. Information gathered should then be fed into the planning process. Managers also need to know the status of negotiations with non-EC countries that their organisation trades with, invests in, faces competition from or originates from.

STEP 2: Identify the most significant changes for your business(es) and conduct a 1992 audit

Obviously, not all the legislation will have a direct, or even indirect, impact on your organisation. The EC standards for motor vehicle manufacturing will not be of great significance to a pharmaceutical company, for instance. However, for example, to car manufacturers and their suppliers, the harmonisation of standards could:

- entail new legally required procedures
- be threatening in particular Member States
- provide new marketing opportunities
- allow cost savings in terms of reducing the number of models that currently need to be manufactured to adhere to 12 different product standards
- allow cost savings in terms of the increased possibilities of trans-frontier joint ventures for research and development
- entail increased costs if the harmonised EC standards are above those currently required in the national home market.

It is clear, therefore, that the key legislative changes for your organisation must be identified.

STEP 3: Review the likely impact of 1992 on potential and existing customers

Existing customers may have changing demands due to their 1992 strategies. In addition, there may be opportunities to service existing clients in a more cost-effective way, through new distribution channels.

1992 could also provide an opportunity for reaching new geographic markets. Market research may be useful to determine the customer profile, distribution points, and competitor activity.

STEP 4: Review the likely impact of 1992 on suppliers

There may be new sources of suppliers in the single market. Suppliers, previously facing costly barriers to enter, could become more price competitive and this could enable organisations to reduce their costs.

STEP 5: Review the likely impact of 1992 on your organisation's present competitors and their likely response

The competition may not be standing still faced with 1992. Many companies are using 1992 as an impetus for change, and thereby finding competitive advantage. Managers should ensure that they monitor competitors' activity.

STEP 6: Examine the possibilities of new entrants to your market

Organisations may also face new competition from emerging competitors. Just as the other Member States' markets will become more accessible to the UK, so the UK market will become more accessible to non-UK companies.

STEP 7: Appraise the opportunities which may arise to sell products or services in new markets

Managers should actively examine strengths and weaknesses. There may be the opportunity for strategic positioning of goods or services in other Member States. Management must also decide how to assess the viability of entering new markets. The process must start with an assessment of the viability, and go through all the steps including the decision as to whether to buy into new markets (through acquisition) or to set up test sites.

STEP 8: Develop and implement a strategy to meet the challenges ahead

Having assessed the likely effects of 1992, a strategic plan can then be developed based on the likely opportunities and threats that the SEM implies for particular sectors.

7 Conclusion

The prospect for the UK of being part of an integrated domestic market of 320 million consumers is drawing closer. The European Commission has already implemented many measures, and more are in the pipeline, to ensure that the Single European Market envisaged by the leading six members and reapplied in 1987 by the twelve, becomes a practical reality in 1992.

Managers should, after reading this book, be acutely aware that the Single European Market is an exciting if complex challenge. The following Checklist for Action (see Appendix I) may help in the process of "gearing up" for 1992. Treated positively, 1992 should be the catalyst for change and restructuring in order to survive in the increasingly competitive industrial and commercial climate that the 1990s will demand of organisations.

Appendix I

Checklist for Action

1 Conduct 1992 audit.

2 Appoint a senior manager responsible for ensuring that all EC legislation is monitored.

3 Arrange that senior managers are regularly briefed about developments concerning the SEM.

4 Communicate the importance of the changes and the need to "think Europe" down the line.

5 Review organisational structure in the light of the SEM.

6 Check productivity and services you offer. Are they good enough?

7 Appoint someone in Personnel to monitor changes in EC employment and related legislation.

8 Review recruiting policies and procedures in the light of proposed moves to free movement of labour and the mutual recognition within EC of professional qualifications.

9 Audit current language skills and review future requirements.

10 Review your organisation's location in the context of the enlarged SEM.

Appendix II

European Community Directives from Start to Finish

The Consultation Procedure

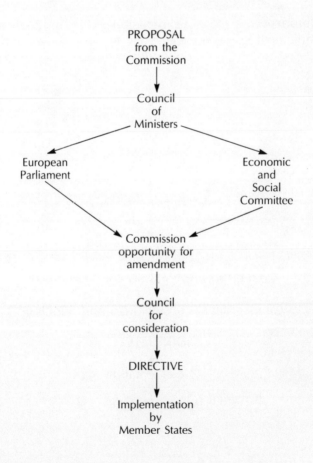

The Co-operation Procedure

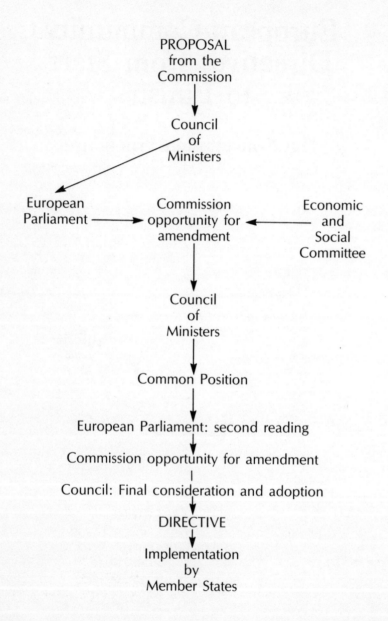

PROPOSAL
from the
Commission

Council
of
Ministers

European   Commission   Economic
Parliament ────────► opportunity for ◄──────── and
                            amendment   Social
                                                         Committee

Council
of
Ministers

Common Position

European Parliament: second reading

Commission opportunity for amendment

Council: Final consideration and adoption

DIRECTIVE

Implementation
by
Member States

Appendix III

European Documentation Centres in the UK

The European Documentation Centres are extremely valuable regional sources of information on the Community. Based at Institutes of Higher Education, they all stock the Official Journal, which lists all Community tenders as well as copies of draft legislation/Directives. Other important documents relating to many Community aspects can also be found at these centres.

ABERDEEN
The Library
University of Aberdeen
Meston Walk
Aberdeen AB9 2UB
Tel: 0224 40241 x 2787

KENT
Library
Wye College
Wye
Ashford'
Kent TN25 5AH
Tel: 0233 812401 x 497

BATH
University Library
University of Bath
Claverton Down
Bath BA2 7AY
Tel: 0225 826826 x 5594

BELFAST
The Library
Government Publications Dept

Queens University
Belfast
Northern Ireland BT7 1LS
Tel: 0232 245133 x 3605

BIRMINGHAM
William Kendrick Library
Birmingham Polytechnic
Birmingham B42 2SU
Tel: 021-331 5289

Main Library
University of Birmingham
PO Box 363
Birmingham B15 2TT
Tel: 021-414 5823

BRADFORD
J.B. Priestley Library
University of Bradford
Richmond Road
Bradford BD7 1DP
Tel: 0274 733466 x 8263

BRIGHTON
The Library
University of Sussex
Brighton BN1 9QL
Tel: 0273 678159

BRISTOL
Law Library
University of Bristol
Queens Road
Bristol BS8 1RJ
Tel: 0272 303370

CAMBRIDGE
The Library
University of Cambridge
West Road
Cambridge CB3 9DR
Tel: 0223 333138

CARDIFF
Arts and Social Studies Library
University College
PO Box 430
Cardiff CF1 3XT
Tel: 0222 8744262

CHALFONT
The Buckinghamshire College
  of Higher Education
Newland Park
Gorelands Lane
Chalfont St. Giles HP8 44D
Tel: 02405 4441 x 245

COLCHESTER
The Library
University of Essex
PO Box 24
Colchester CO4 3UA
Tel: 0206 862286

COLERAINE
The Library
New University of Ulster
Coleraine BT52 1SA
Tel: 0265 4141 x 257

COVENTRY
The Library
Lanchester Polytechnic
Priory Street
Coventry CV1 2HF
Tel: 0203 24166 x 2452/2698

The Library
University of Warwick
Coventry CV4 7A
Tel: 0203 523523 x 2041

DUNDEE
University of Dundee
Perth Road
Dundee DD1 4HN
Tel: 0382 23181 x 4101

DURHAM
Official Publications Section
University Library
Stockton Road
Durham DH1 3LY
Tel: 091-374 3041

EDINBURGH
Centre of European
  Government Studies
University of Edinburgh
Old College
South Bridge
Edinburgh EH8 9LY
Tel: 031-667 1011 x 4215

ESSEX
Essex Institute of Higher
   Education
Victoria Road South
Chelmsford
Essex CM1 1LL
Tel: 0245 493131

EXETER
Centre for European Legal
   Studies
Exeter Building (Law Faculty)
Amory Building
Rennes Drive
Exeter EX4 4RJ
Tel: 0392 263356

GLASGOW
The University Library
University of Glasgow
Hillhead Street
Glasgow G12 8QE
Tel: 041-339 8855 x 6744

GUILDFORD
George Edwards Library
University of Surrey
Guildford GU2 5XH
Tel: 0483 509233

HULL
Brynmor Jones Library
University of Hull
Cottingham Road
Hull HU6 7RX
Tel: 0482 465441

KEELE
The Library
University of Keele
Keele
Staffs ST5 5RG
Tel: 0782 621111 x 3737

KENT
Library Building
University of Kent
Canterbury
Kent CT2 7NU
Tel: 0227 66822

LANCASTER
University of Lancaster Library
Lancaster LA1 4YX
Tel: 0524 65201 x 276

LEEDS
The Library
Leeds Polytechnic
Calverley Street
Leeds LS1 3HE
Tel: 0532 462925

LEICESTER
University of Leeds
20 Lyddon Terrace
Leeds LS7 9JT
Tel: 0532 31751

LIVERPOOL
University Library
University of Leicester
University Road
Leicester LE1 7RH
Tel: 0533 522044

LONDON
Liverpool and District Science
  and Industry Research
  Council
Central Libraries
William Brown Street
Liverpool L3 8EW
Tel: 051-207 2147 x 45

The Library
Queen Mary College
Mile End Road
London E1 4NS
Tel: 01-980 4811 x 3307

The Library
Polytechnic of North London
Prince of Wales Road
London NW5
Tel: 01-359 0941

British Library
English Collection
Great Russell Street
London WC1B 3DB
Tel: 01-323 7602

The Library
R11A
10 St. James Square
London SW1Y 4LE
Tel: 01-930 2233 x 260

European Depository Library
Central Reference Library
City of Westminster Library
St. Martins Street
London WC2 7HP
Tel: 01-798 3131

British Library of Political and
  Economic Science
The Library
10 Portugal Street
London WC2A 2HD
Tel: 01-405 7686 x 2993

LOUGHBOROUGH
The Library
Loughborough University of
  Technology
Loughborough LE11 3TU
Tel: 0509 222344

MANCHESTER
John Rylands Library
University of Manchester
Oxford Road
Manchester M13 9PP
Tel: 061-273 3333

NEWCASTLE-UPON-TYNE
The Library
Newcastle Polytechnic
Ellison Place
Newcastle-upon-Tyne NE1 8ST
Tel: 091-275 3727

NORWICH
The Library
University of East Anglia
University Plain
Norwich NR4 7TJ
Tel: 0603 56161 x 2412

NOTTINGHAM
The Library
University of Nottingham
Nottingham NG7 2RD
Tel: 0602 506101 x 3741

54

OXFORD
Bodleian Library
University of Oxford
Oxford OX1 3BG
Tel: 0865 277201

PORTSMOUTH
Frewen Library
Portsmouth Polytechnic
Cambridge Road
Portsmouth PO1 2ST
Tel: 0705 277201

READING
The Library
University of Reading
Whiteknights
PO Box 223
Reading RG6 2AH
Tel: 0734 874331 x 131

SALFORD
The Library
University of Salford
Salford M5 4WT
Tel: 061 736 5843 x 7218

SHEFFIELD
The Library
Sheffield City Polytechnic
Pond Street
Sheffield S1 1WB
Tel: 0742 20911 x 2494

SOUTHAMPTON
Faculty of Law
University of Southampton
Southampton SO9 5NH
Tel: 0703 559122 x 3451

WESTERBY
British Library
Document Supply Centre
Boston Spa
Westerby LS23 7BQ
Tel: 0937 843434 x 6035

WOLVERHAMPTON
Robert Scott Library
Polytechnic of Wolverhampton
St. Peters Square
Wolverhampton WV1 1RH
Tel: 0902 313005 x 2300

Appendix IV

Other Sources of Information

General information on EC matters can be obtained from the Commission's UK offices.

These are found at:

8 Storey's Gate
London SW1P 3AT
Tel: 01-222 8122

Windsor House
9–15 Bedford Street
Belfast BT2 7EG
Tel: 40708

4 Cathedral Road
Cardiff CF1 9JG
Tel: 37 1631

7 Alva Street
Edinburgh EH2 4PH
Tel: 225 2058

A basic library about the Community is available free from any Commission office:

1 *Working Together* – by Emile Noel, Secretary-General of the Commission. A 40-page guide to the institutions of the Community and how they work.
2 *Steps to European Unity* – a chronological account of the Community's origins and development.
3 *Britain in the EC – The Impact of Membership* – a detailed

summary of developments since 1972. Covers most areas of policy; particularly strong on trade, industry, agriculture and legislation. Regional versions for Northern Ireland, Scotland, Wales and the major English regions are available and contain much additional detailed material. They can be consulted at any Commission office. All are being revised.

4 *One Parliament for Ten* – The European Parliament – its powers, groupings, committees, etc. Colour.

5 *About Europe* – a substantial, illustrated booklet examining many Community policies.

6 *Finance from Europe* – detailed guide to Community funds.

7 *The EC as a Publisher* – 80-page pocket catalogue of material about the Community, by subject.

8 *Europe at a Glance* – a brief guide to the Community and Britain's share in its activities.

9 *Scotland in Europe* and *Questions and Answers* (Wales) are available free from the Commission's offices in Edinburgh and Cardiff respectively.

NOTE: Multiple copies of the last two series of pamphlets may be available for seminars, etc.

A useful pack on TED (Tenders Electronic Daily) is free from any Commission office.

Information about the European Parliament may be obtained from the European Parliament Information Office:

2 Queen Anne's Gate
London SW1H 9AA
Tel: 01-222 0411

They have a library containing information on the Parliament's proceedings and produce a free monthly newsletter *European Parliament News*.

Information can also be obtained from the DTI:

1–19 Victoria Street
London
SW1H 0ET
The DTI Hotline: 01 200 1992

The DTI also publishes a booklet and information pack on the Single European Market programme: *An Introduction to the Single European Market*. This is available free from the DTI; just telephone the Hotline. The booklet is to be regularly updated. They have also published an action checklist for business: *Towards 1992*, which is short, relevant and a good guide as to how to tackle the SEM strategically.

Two videos made by the DTI are also available:

1 *Europe Open for Business* – a 12-minute introduction to the SEM – this video can be obtained from the DTI.
2 A more practically based video of 10 minutes duration based on an imaginary case study of a company working up to the SEM can be obtained from:

CFL Vision
PO Box 35
Wetherby
Yorkshire LS23 7EX
Tel: 0937 844524

Hire rate: £9.99
To buy: £118.99 (inc VAT, postage and packing)

Spearhead is DTI's on-line database of vital Single Market information. It summarises the current and prospective European Community measures which will mean change for businesses between now and 1992, and gives access to the full texts of relevant Community legislation. Spearhead can be accessed through Profile Information, a part of the "Financial Times" Group. It can be dialled, directly by subscribers to Profile, on the ordinary telephone.

Information on exporting to different EC Countries may be obtained by ringing the following numbers:

For exporting to:	Ring:
Belgium, Luxembourg	01 215 5886
Denmark	01 215 5140
France	01 215 4762
West Germany	01 215 4796
Greece	01 215 4776
Eire	01 215 4783
Italy	01 215 5103
Netherlands	01 215 4790
Portugal	01 215 5307
Spain	01 215 4260
General enquiries	01 215 5549

Information on collaborative R & D projects may be obtained from:

The UK EUREKA Office
DTI
Room 204
Ashdown House
123 Victoria Street
London SW1E 6RB

SMEs can obtain information and advice at the Centres for European Business Information.

These are found at:

Centre for European Business Information
Small Firms Service
Ebury Bridge Road
2–18 Ebury Bridge Road
London SW1W 8QD
Tel: 01-730 8155

Birmingham Chamber of Industry and Commerce
75 Harborne Road
Birmingham B15 3DH
Tel: 021-454 6171

Newcastle Polytechnic Library
Ellison Building
Ellison Place
Newcastle NE1 8ST
Tel: 091-232 6002

Strathclyde Euro Info Centre
25 Bothwell Street
Glasgow G2 6NR
Tel: 041-221 0999

The Industrial Society is closely monitoring the SEM's progress and is a useful point of reference. Contact:

The Europe Campaign Leader
International Department
48 Bryanston Square
London W1
Tel: 01–262 2401

Ernst & Winney have worked closely with the Commission on the 1992 initiative and can provide information and advice. Please contact Malcolm Levitt at:

Becket House
1 Lambeth Palace Road
London SE1 7EU
tel: 01–928 2000

Published books on Europe and the Single European Market:

Europe – Update '88, Discussion Paper No. 10, published by The British Institute of Management, Management House, Cottingham Road, Corby, Northants NN17 11TT, (tel: 0536 20422), £9.50. A useful guide to the current state of play regarding the 300 Directives. 47 pages.

The EEC – A Guide to the Maze, S.A. Budd, published by Kogan Page, £6.95. A detailed guide to how the Community works. 209 pages.

Europe 1992 Developing an Active Company Approach to the European Market, J. Drew and E.V. Drew, Whurr Publications, (tel: 226 1729). A guide on how organisations should approach the SEM strategically.